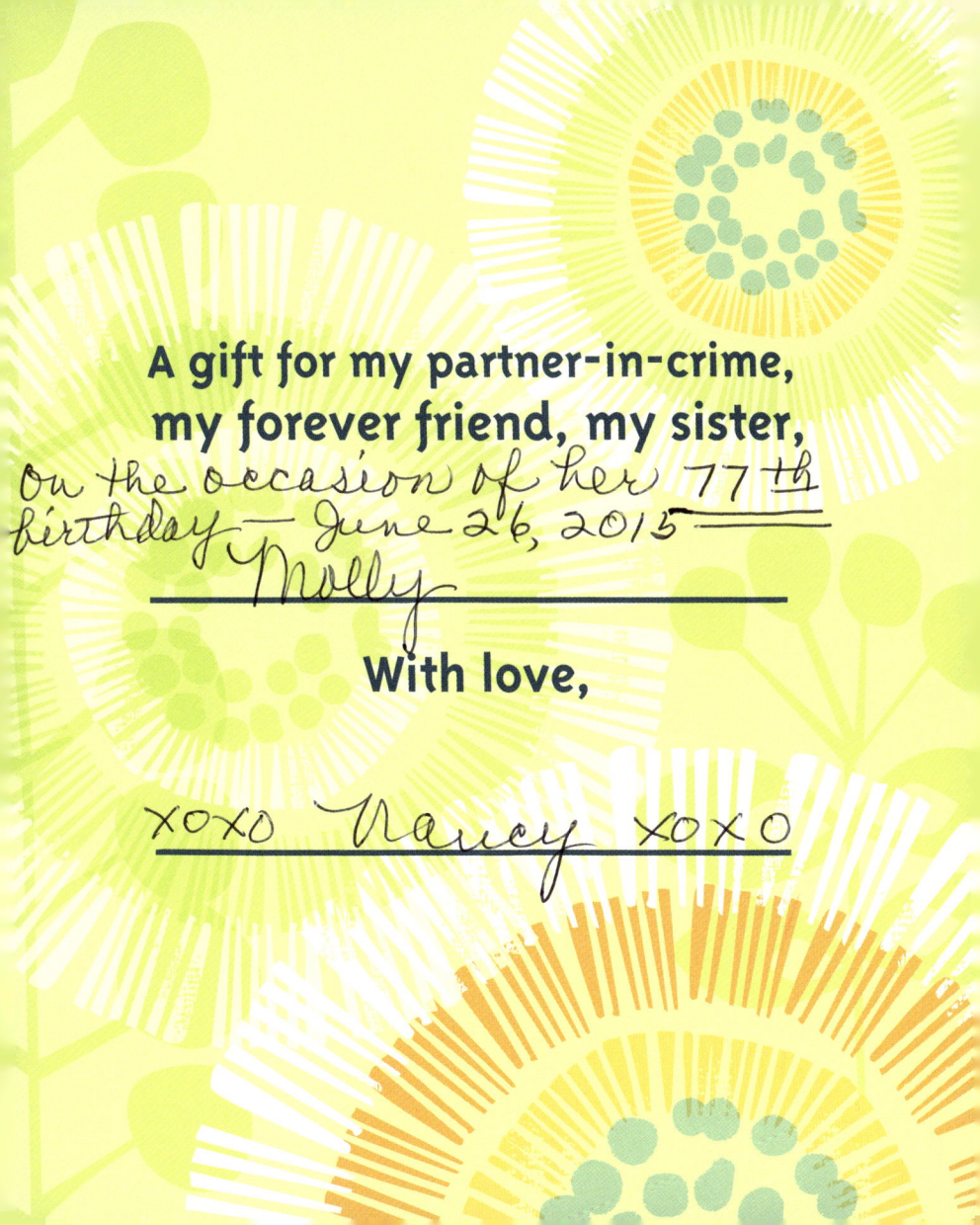

A gift for my partner-in-crime, my forever friend, my sister, On the occasion of her 77th birthday — June 26, 2015
Molly

With love,

xoxo Nancy xoxo

Copyright © 2014 Hallmark Licensing, LLC

Published by Hallmark Gift Books,
a division of Hallmark Cards, Inc.,
Kansas City, MO 64141
Visit us on the Web at Hallmark.com.

All rights reserved. No part of this publication may be reproduced, transmitted, or stored in any form or by any means without the prior written permission of the publisher.

Editorial Director: Carrie Bolin
Editor: Kim Schworm Acosta
Art Director: Jan Mastin
Designer: Brian Pilachowski
Production Designer: Dan Horton

ISBN: 978-1-59530-713-2
BOK2171

Printed and bound in China
SEP14

but sometimes, all you really need is your
SISTER.

When I think about all the stuff

we didn't tell mom...

MY
CONFIDANTE
SANITY-SAVER
BAD INFLUENCE
GOOD INFLUENCE
SISTER

A sister . . .

the one who stands by you through thick and thin . . .

and slightly pudgy.

For all the things

you've talked me into

and the things

you've talked me out of . . .

I love you.

We've done it all—

FOUGHT, MADE UP,
TATTLED, KEPT SECRETS, COMPETED, TEAMED UP—

but no matter what,
I've never felt I had to
face the world alone.

Time passes.
Sisters hang in there with you.

Life is just better that way.

EVEN WHEN SOMEONE IRRITATES THE CRAP OUT OF YOU, you can still love them.

Sisters teach us that.

That's why having you for a sister was **so much fun.** Still is.

A sister is a best friend with a

LIFETIME
GUARANTEE.

There's no one like a sister

to point out what's wrong with you and praise what's right about you

all in the same sentence.

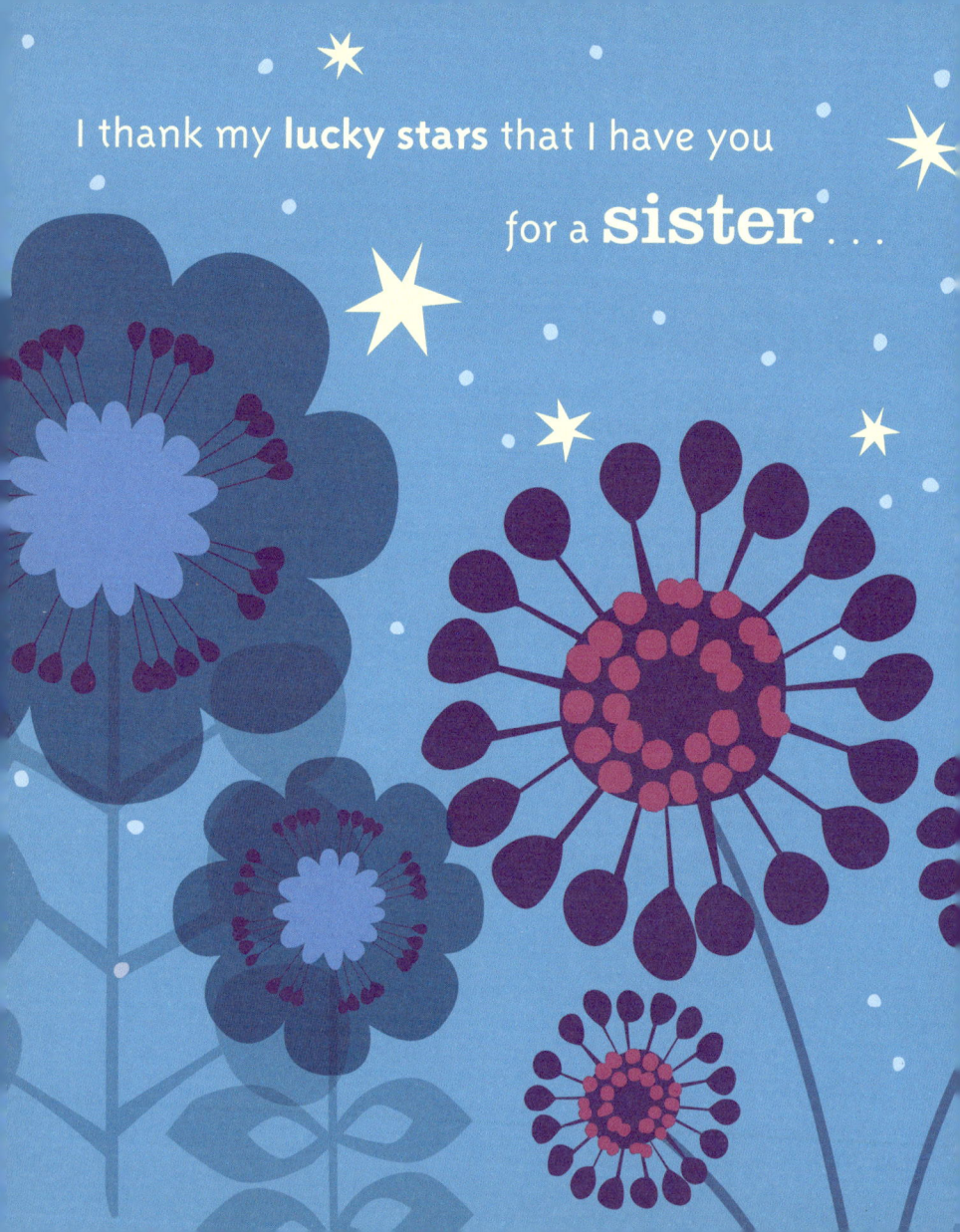

But since I don't know exactly which stars are my lucky ones, I just kind of look up in the sky and say thanks, trusting that my lucky stars know who they are.

Woven into the fabric of childhood

are the **colorful memories**

sisters share.

A sister is **the first** one to call you when you post something online that she didn't already know about.

You don't have to explain

much to a sister.

She can **read your heart**.

You keep my secrets,
and I keep yours.
It's a beautiful thing…

and **AMAZING,**
considering what
little tattletales
we used to be.

A sister remembers you **when**

knows you **now**,

and loves you

just the way you are.

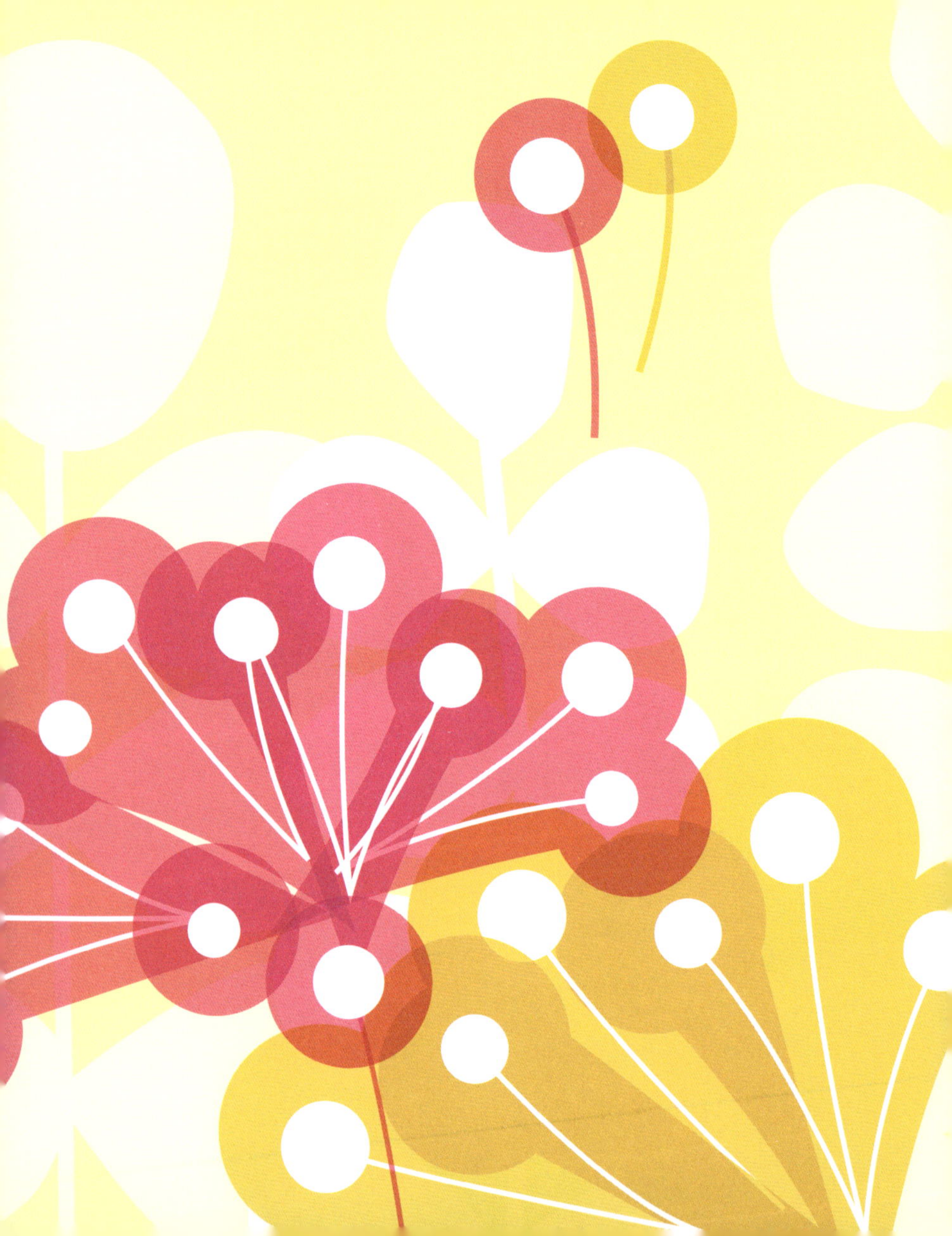

You wouldn't think a person could be talked into trading the good stuff in her Halloween haul for a bunch of candy corn, but there's A SISTER for you.

SISTER LOVE is nothing
to mess with.
Sister love isn't made out of
cupcakes and glitter.
More like steel and
a set of snow tires.
It went the extra mile
a long while back,
and it's not going to quit,
not tomorrow,
NOT EVER.

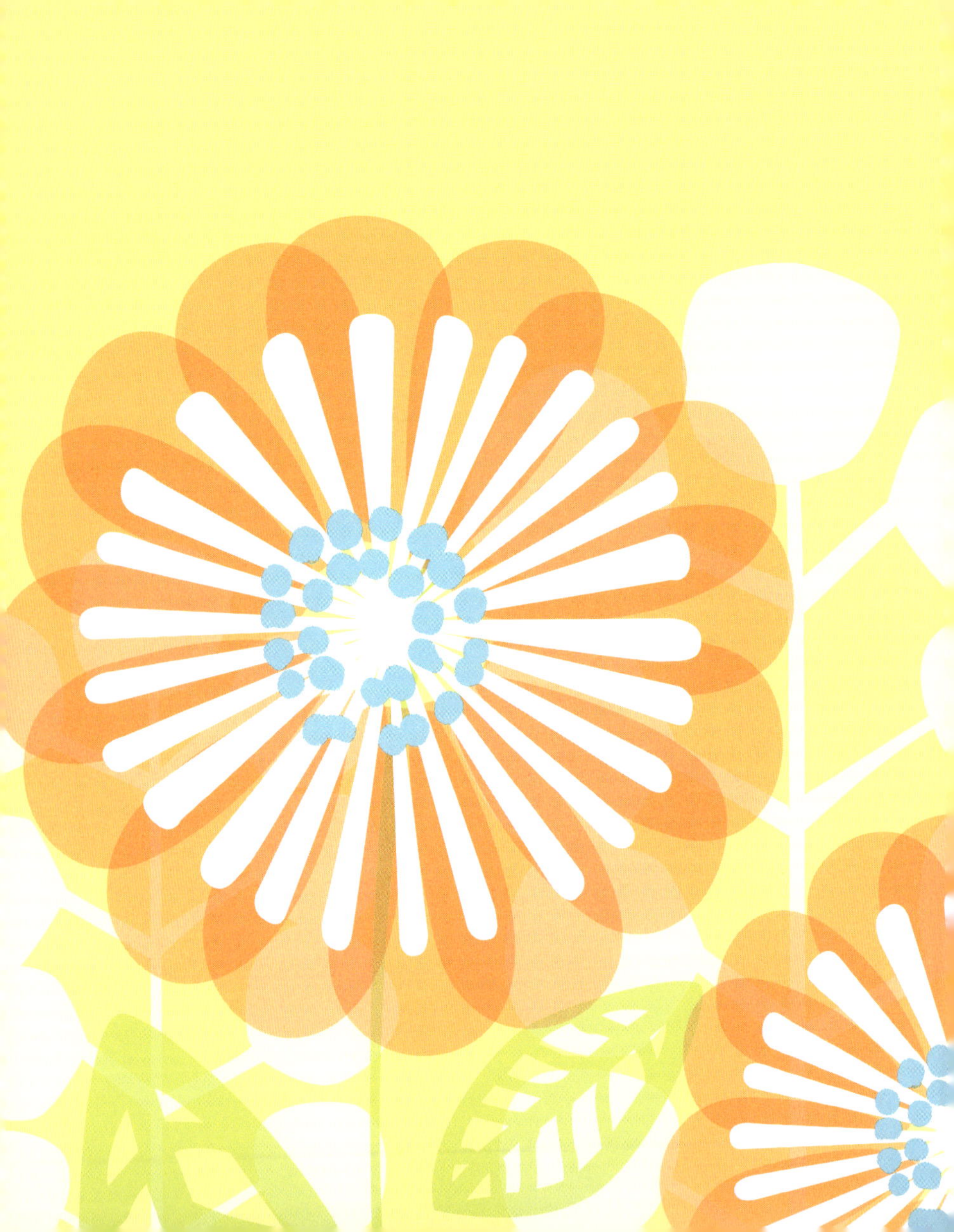

AMAZING

She was there for the beginning.

She was there for the good parts

(and the not-so-good parts).

And she'll be there for what's to come.

SISTER

A **girl** I knew back when.
A **woman** I've come to admire.
A **friend** who's always there . . .

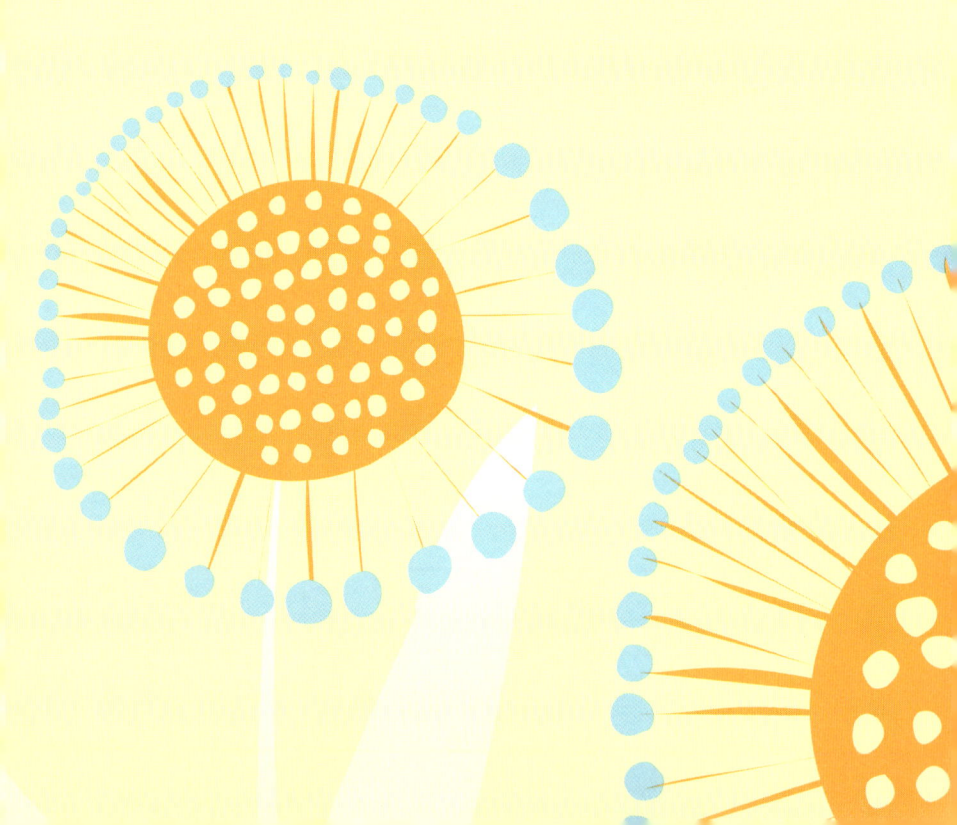

A **sister** I'll always love.

You're the BEST SISTER anyone could ask for . . .

even though I don't remember ever asking for one.

When you have a sister,
you're part of
an unforgettable team...

the best possible combination of
friend & family.

Only sisters know the thin line **between HUG and STRANGLE.**

Lipstick, mascara,
secrets, dreams,
that pair of earrings
(you know the ones). . .

Of all the things we've shared,
our friendship is my favorite.

Because you're my sister
and my friend . . .

I'm twice blessed.

As a kid, I spent a lot of time wishing you'd **GET LOST**. Now, I spend a lot of time wishing you **lived next door**.

We didn't just **grow up** together.

We grew **fabulous** together.

When your sister's got your back,

there's only one direction to go.

Forward.

Growing up is tough for everyone.
But thankfully, I had a sister
to help me discover
THE SMART WAY,
THE COOL WAY,
THE JUST-BE-YOU WAY
to get through it all.

There is **one kind** of laugh

you can only laugh

with a sister.

Through the good, the bad, and the **"YOU HAVE GOT TO BE KIDDING ME,"** a sister is always there.

A sister knows when to listen,
when to stop listening,
when to talk,
when to stop talking,
when to pour wine,
when to stop pouring

AND JUST HAND OVER THE BOTTLE.

A sister is someone who knows you better than Amazon and Netflix **COMBINED.**

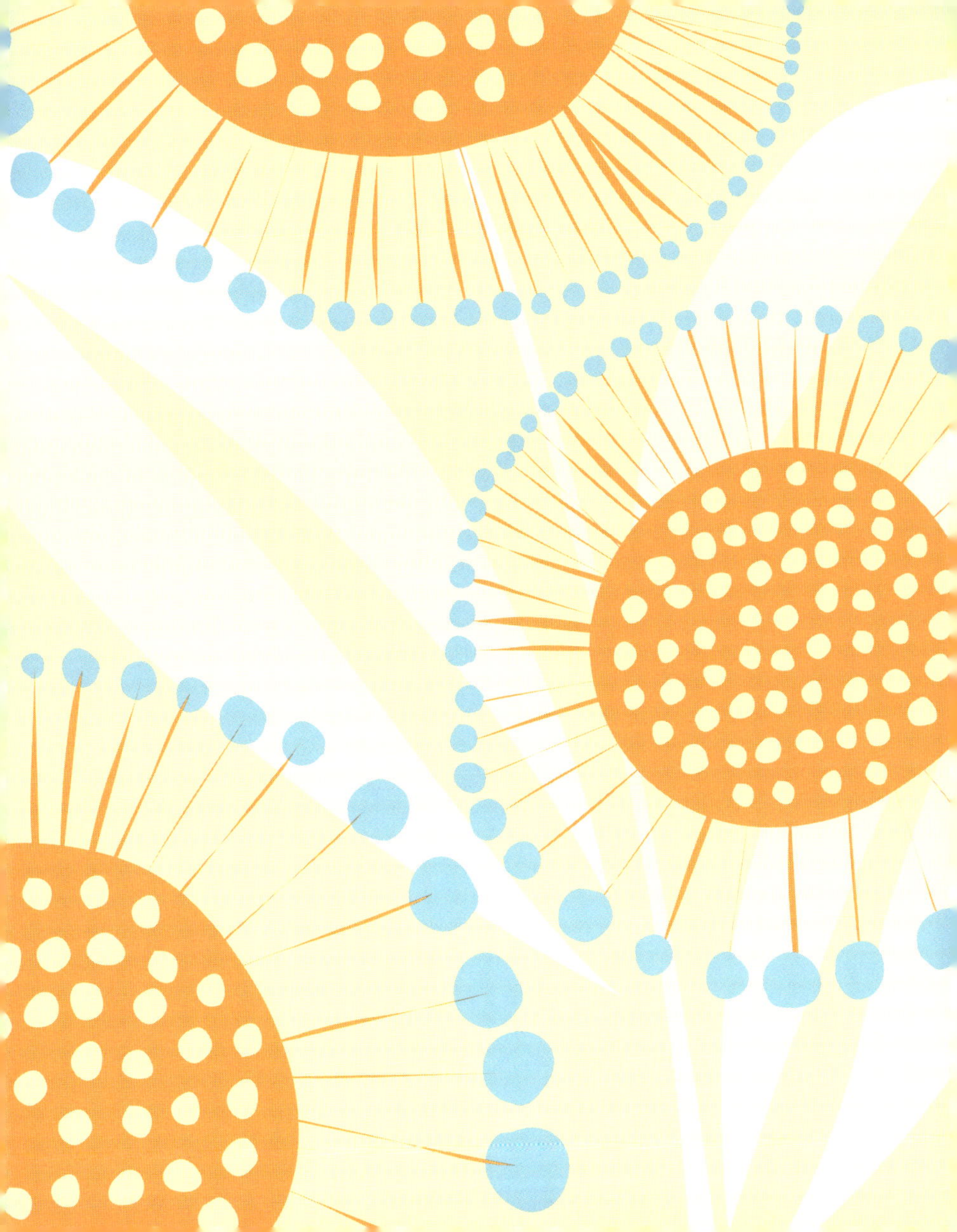

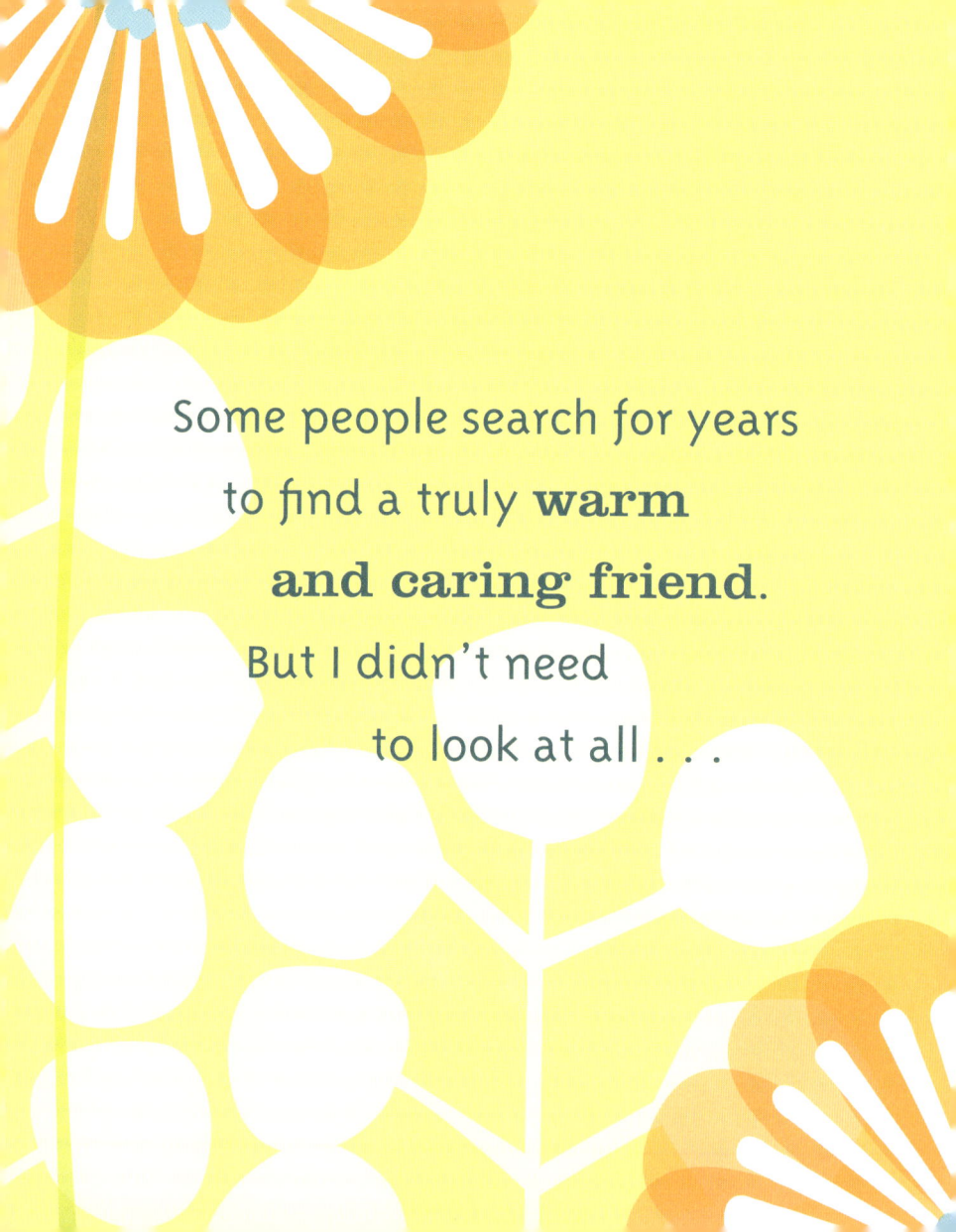

Some people search for years
to find a truly **warm
and caring friend**.
But I didn't need
to look at all . . .

I had one right
    in my own family.

If you and your sister
enjoyed this book,
or it has touched your life in
some way, we would love to
hear from you.

Please send your comments to:
Hallmark Book Feedback
P.O. Box 419034
Mail Drop 100
Kansas City, MO 64141

Or e-mail us at:
booknotes@hallmark.com